So You Love to Draw

So You Love to Draw

Every Kid's Guide to Becoming an Artist

By Michael Seary

Illustrations by Michel Bisson

Douglas & McIntyre

Vancouver / Toronto / Buffalo

For Marion

My thanks go to Maria Martella of the Children's Book Store in Toronto, whose encouragement helped me to start this exploration; to many children in Halifax at the Art Gallery of Nova Scotia, and in Toronto and Orangeville, Ontario; and to Eduard Kodar, who read the manuscript and gave valuable suggestions.

DOUGLAS & MCINTYRE
585 Bloor Street West
Toronto, Ontario M6G 1K5

Distributed in the U.S. by
PUBLISHERS GROUP WEST
4065 Hollis Street,
Emeryville CA 94608

Canadian Cataloguing in Publication Data

Seary, Michael
    So you love to draw: every kids guide to becoming an artist

ISBN 1-55054-238-9

1. Drawing - Technique - Juvenile literature.
I. Bisson, Michel. II. Title.

NC655.S43 1996   j741.2   C96-930042-5

The publisher gratefully acknowledges the assistance of the Canada Council and of the British Columbia Ministry of Tourism, Small Business and Culture.

Design: Michael Solomon

Contents

I

Getting Started

You Can Be an Artist

We are all artists. You've been one ever since you were a baby scribbling with a crayon. In kindergarten you probably made dozens of pictures of your family, trucks, rainbows, or whatever else caught your interest.

We can all draw and paint, sculpt and construct. Some of us take to art more readily than others, but everyone gets better with practice. That is what this book is about: improving your skills as an artist with practice—the practice of art.

With enough practice, you might even earn money being an artist. Some artists paint pictures that people buy to hang in their homes or offices, or in art galleries. But there are many other kinds of artists, too. Graphic artists make designs and diagrams that are used in advertising or in science, engineering or medicine. (For example, the big poster of a tooth hanging in your dentist's office was designed by a graphic artist.) Illustrators draw pictures for magazines, posters or books like this one. Some illustrators even do their work on computers instead of with a pen or paintbrush.

"But I can't draw!"

When people say this, they usually mean that they want to be able to draw better. Often they want to be able to make a picture look more life-like, the way a photograph of a dog looks just like the real animal. Most artists who can draw like this have practiced for many years.

But what about the rest of us?

Can we all learn to do a presentable drawing of something, even if we are not necessarily gifted?

Answer these questions:
● Do you like to draw?
● Are you willing to practice in order to improve?
● Do you want to explore new ways of doing art?

If you answered yes to these three questions, you can be an artist. Read on.

As you progress in art there will probably be times when you get discouraged. Everyone does. Painters, musicians, dancers, athletes and actors all have to practice. They all get discouraged, but they also have the satisfaction of improving their skills, and some of them reach the top.

Nature artist Robert Bateman works on a number of pictures at the same time. That way, when he gets discouraged with one painting, he can work on another one instead.

Humans have always been artists. Twenty thousand years ago, our stone age ancestors drew pictures of animals and hunters on the walls of caves. Five hundred years ago, painters like Leonardo, Raphael and Michelangelo filled their sketchbooks with figures, scenes and designs. Today art is everywhere—in magazines, on billboards, on television, in galleries and on the walls of buildings.

What You Need

Work Space

As an artist, you need a place to work. This is your studio.

Ideally your studio will have these things:

● Some privacy so you will be able to concentrate—perhaps your room, or a quiet corner away from distractions.

● Good light, including, if possible, daylight from a north-facing window. This will give you plenty of even light, but the sun won't shine directly on your work.

● A flat, smooth surface such as a table or desk. Some artists like to prop up a large piece of plywood or masonite at a slight angle. This stops you from hunching over your work and straining your neck and shoulders.

● Display space. You'll want a bulletin board or wall space where you can tack up your pictures. You can learn a lot by studying your own art.

● A storage place for your art and your supplies. You'll probably need a box or drawer for pencils, pens, brushes, inks and paints. Art materials can be expensive, so artists take good care of their tools. And you should have a portfolio to put your art in. You can make a simple one by folding a large piece of cardboard in half. After each practice session, put your best drawings in the folder. Be sure to date each one (see page 62 for more information on saving and displaying your work).

Pencils

Artists use many different tools to do their work, but to start, all you really need is a pencil and paper. There are many kinds of pencils, but an ordinary HB or 2B pencil is fine to start with. You probably have some of these at home.

Don't worry about whether your pencil has a little eraser on the end. They just get hard or wear down, and usually end up smudging your work or tearing the paper. Try to have a soft eraser that removes pencil marks cleanly and completely. (Besides, artists don't always erase lines from a sketch as they are drawing. Instead, they use these lines as a guide to more satisfactory ones.)

Sketch Pads

Every artist needs a sketch pad to jot down ideas for pictures, to practice drawing, to record things. It doesn't have to be fancy or expensive. Any unlined paper attached to a clip board is fine to start.

● Your sketch pad should be small enough that you can carry it around with you—no larger than a school notebook.

● It should have a firm back so that you can draw standing up. (You might want to sketch something you see while you're sitting on the bus, or while you're on a walk.)

● The paper should be thick enough that a drawing doesn't show through on the back.

Many artists sketch every day. They do this to "keep their hand in"—keep their drawing skills sharp. Sketching also helps them to remember and record the things they see each day.

Life is busy. You've got to fit in school, hockey practices, meals, piano lessons and hanging-out time. Maybe there's no way you'll be able to sketch every single day. Don't worry. Art is a bit like exercise. We're told that a half-hour workout three times a week will still keep you in shape. Well, in art, even one sketch a week is better than nothing. Remember to date each sketch. Write down what the sketch is and where it was done, too.

As a schoolboy, Alfred Pellan spent much of his time sketching secretly in the margins of his notebooks. He sketched on Monday, Tuesday, Wednesday and Thursday. On Friday, he had art class. Pellan did not do well in school, but he became one of Quebec's outstanding artists.

Pencil leads are usually graded from very hard to very soft by the letters H or B combined with a number. (The letter H comes from the German word *hart*, meaning hard; B comes from the word *blei*, meaning lead.) You'll usually find the letters stamped right on the pencil. A 4H pencil is very hard, a 4B pencil is very soft, and an HB pencil is medium. Artists often use a hard pencil when they want to show detail, because the pencil holds a sharp point and makes a fine line. Soft pencils make heavier lines that can vary in thickness.

Collect a number of pencils from around the house and experiment with them, drawing lines of different thicknesses and weights. See which pencil lines erase more easily. Then choose the pencil that suits you best.

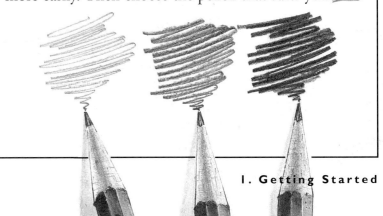

Warming Up

You have your sketch pad. You've printed your name and address on it in case you lose it. Now you are ready to sketch.

Many artists like to warm up before they start to draw. Maybe you already do this in the margins of notebooks or telephone pads. It's called doodling, and it helps you free your imagination.

Warm-up exercises can be loose or tight. Loose drawings are free-flowing and relaxed. Tight drawings are careful and controlled, sometimes small, with lots of detail. Artists want to be able to draw both loosely and tightly when they need to. So they do some warm-up exercises to loosen up and some to tighten up, the same way athletes do stretching and muscle-building exercises to get in shape before a race or game.

Warm-up Drawings

Use an ordinary pencil for these drawings:

● Draw many kinds of lines. Make straight lines, squiggly ones, thick, thin, long, short, jagged, swirling and wandering lines. Fill a whole page with them.

● Use lines to draw different kinds of shapes:
- regular shapes like circles, squares, triangles, ovals, parallelograms, diamonds
- free-flowing shapes like clouds, lakes and rivers as seen from an airplane, patterns like the ones frost leaves on the window, shadows on the pavement
- shapes of things like hearts, flowers, leaves, teardrops
- crazy shapes that are jagged, swirling or full of holes like Swiss cheese

● Fill in spaces between shapes with a scribble technique.

● Use dots or little tiny squares to make patterns.

● Draw continuous wavy lines without lifting your pencil from the paper.

● Draw over the top of a previous doodle, perhaps with a colored pencil.

From the age of eight, Beatrix Potter made her own sketchbooks by stitching together odd sheets of paper. In these she drew birds, flowers, butterflies, cottages and animals, usually in careful detail. Sometimes she added a touch of fantasy, such as a rabbit walking upright. "I cannot resist, I must draw, however poor the result," she once wrote in her diary. In 1901, when she was thirty-three years old, Peter Rabbit *was published.*

Observation and Memory

To be an artist, you need to train your hand to draw what your eye sees and your brain remembers. This means you need good observation and memory skills.

Artists look closely at things. They observe the size of objects in relation to each other, their outline shapes, their colors, patterns, textures and shadows. A good memory is especially useful when you can't draw something you see right away. For example, you might notice an interesting scene while you're sitting in the car or on the bus. If you have a good memory, you'll be able to remember the details of the scene and draw it later.

Memory Teaser
Try this alone or with a friend. You'll need a piece of paper, a watch or kitchen timer, and a pencil.

Walk into any room. Set the timer for two minutes. Look around you, noting as many different things as you can.

When the two minutes are up, leave the room. Try to picture the room and its contents in your mind. Make a list of what you saw.

Return to the room. What did you miss? Which items were easy to remember? Which ones did you forget? Why were they not memorable? If you remembered colors, were they the right ones? Did you remember details, such as the shape of the knobs on a cabinet, or the leaves on a plant?

Drawing from Memory
The next time you're waiting for your parents at the mall, or waiting for the school bus to pull out, imagine that you have just spotted a suspicious-looking car. Observe the make, color, number of doors and headlights, size of windows, licence plate, nicks and rust spots. Try to draw the car from memory. Then compare it with the real car, unless the owner has driven it away!

You can also try this exercise with birds. Spot a bird on your lawn or feeder. Notice the shape of the head, the size of the head compared to the body, the shape of the beak and tail, the colors and markings. Then whip out your sketch pad and try to draw the bird from memory. Compare your drawing with the real bird, or a picture in a bird guide.

A famous writer named Gertrude Stein once said, "I like museums. I like to look out their windows." To improve your observation skills, look out your own window and make a list of everything you see framed there.

2

Drawing Objects

Drawing Single Objects

The world is full of things to draw, but many of them seem too complicated for a beginner. Sometimes it's hard to know where to start.

To begin, it's easier to draw single objects rather than drawing groups of things or trying to show the background or surface that objects are sitting on.

Drawing from Observation: A Step-by-Step Approach

Look around the room for a simple object to draw. It could be almost anything—a pair of scissors, a hockey puck, the TV set, a model airplane, a doll or toy animal. To become skilled at drawing this object, you'll need to draw it many times, from different views, in different ways. The more you draw, the better your work will become. Use one sheet of paper for each drawing.

● Place your object on a table and look at it carefully. Note its general shape, outline, the size and position of its parts, and how they are connected together. Imagine how the drawing will look on the paper. Move the object into different positions and decide which angle would be the easiest to draw.

● Draw a very light outline, or **contour**, of the object, without adding any details. This is called "blocking in." Roughly sketch important features that would show within the outline (the eyes, nose and mouth on the doll; the buttons and screen on the TV set).

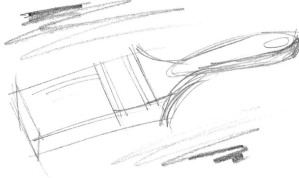

● On top of the outline, lightly draw squares or ovals to simplify the object into its main parts. Show where and how these shapes are joined. Do not erase the original outline drawing. Keep looking at the real object to make sure the angles and proportions of your drawing are the same as those of the object.

● Define the outline using heavier pressure with your pencil. Now add a few details (you might want to do practice drawings of these details before adding them to the big sketch). Choose details that will make your drawing look more lifelike —dials on a radio, a buckle on a belt, little bumps on the surface of a vegetable, fur on a teddy bear.

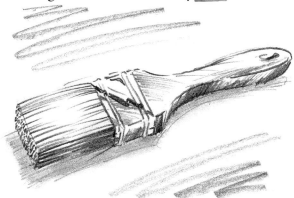

Once you have finished your drawing, do another one, perhaps from a different angle, perhaps emphasizing different details. (Remember that every time you draw something, you are learning to observe the details and proportions more closely.) When you have done a number of sketches, spread them out on the floor and study them carefully. Ask a friend to look at the sketches with you.

● Which drawings do you like best and why?
● Which ones turned out to be better than or different from what you expected?
● Which are not good enough to keep? Why not?
● Which have some good parts and some bad parts? Why do you think some parts are good?
● If you and your friend have made different choices, discuss why.
● Now, date the work you plan to keep and put it in a folder for future reference.

Single Object Experiments

Here are some ways to experiment with drawing a single object. Use a separate piece of paper for each drawing. Again, try not to use an eraser.

● Place the object on a table right at your eye level. Draw the object directly from the front or side.
● Place the object on a low table or the floor and draw it from the top.
● Turn the object so it sits at a bit of an angle and do a drawing that shows the top and two of the sides.
● Draw the object as quickly as you can. Do not go over mistakes with your pencil, and do not rub out any lines. Then do a second drawing, taking as much time as you like. Think about where each line should go before you draw it.
● Draw the object in a continuous line, without lifting your pencil from the paper.
● Draw the object on very light paper, such as tracing paper, using the faintest line possible. Now draw it again on a separate piece of paper using the heaviest line possible (try not to tear the paper!). Make the second drawing the same size and from the same angle as the first. Hold the two drawings up to the light so you can see the dark one behind the light one. How similar are they?
● Cut out the most interesting parts of all the drawings you have just made and glue them onto a piece of colored construction paper to make an interesting pattern.

Bored with the object you've chosen? Pick something else, perhaps an object that especially interests you. Draw a piece of sports equipment, a ballet shoe, a plastic dinosaur or a tire from a racing car. Who knows? Your favorite subject may become a lifetime theme. One Halifax artist has more than forty sketchbooks filled with drawings of the RCMP—Mounties and their horses, hats, saddles and boots.

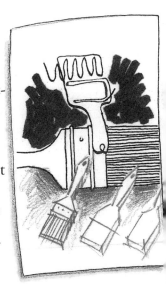

Ink, Chalk, Charcoal and Crayon

So far, all your sketches have probably been drawn with a pencil. But an artist can work with many tools.

Using various pencils, ballpoint pens, felt-tipped pens or markers, crayons, chalks and charcoals can make your drawings look very different.

Inks are liquid solutions that have **pigments** (coloring matter) dissolved in them. There are many ways to apply ink. Fine ballpoint, nylon-tipped or felt-tipped pens or markers are good for drawing thin lines and small details. Thick felt-tipped pens will give you bold lines. Ink can also be applied with a brush, or with a nib pen, for free-flowing lines.

But ink is hard to erase, so artists sometimes start with a pencil. This is the way many comic-book artists work. Once they have worked out or "roughed in" the proper

positions, shapes and contours, they redraw them with ink and add details and textures. Then they erase any pencil lines that still show.

Chalks and charcoals are good for creating shaded areas. **Chalk pastels** (similar to blackboard chalk) contain fine powder. They work best on rough paper (where the powder can fall into the crevices in the paper). **Oil pastels** are like chalk, but they contain "sizing" (glue) to bind the powdered color to the paper.

Some chalks and oil pastels smudge easily (on you or on your art). They are good for mixing colors (for example, you can rub blue on top of yellow to make green). Hard chalks and pastels are better for drawing lines. You can change the width and heaviness of the line by pressing harder, or by using the point or side of the tip.

Charcoals are brittle black sticks made of burnt wood. (There are also pencils that contain charcoal instead of graphite "lead.") Place a piece of thin paper, such as tissue paper, over charcoal drawings to prevent them from smudging.

Artists also use **crayons**, where the pigment is mixed with wax. Crayons work on smooth paper as well as on rough paper. They don't smudge, but they only give you thick lines. You can mix colors, but the colors are less intense than those of chalks or pastels.

Eventually, you'll probably want to buy different kinds of art materials, but for now just use the pens, chalks or crayons that you find around the house.

Different Tools, Different Effects

Using several art materials, try some of the warm-up experiments on page 10. See what different effects you can achieve. Now choose a simple subject—a school bag, a jug, a bunch of bananas, a bicycle helmet or a baseball glove.

● First, sketch your subject in pencil. When you are satisfied with the shape of the object, add some details. Show the thickness of the rim of the jug, the broken stem at the end of the bananas, the strap of the bike helmet, the stitching on the glove.

● With pen and ink or ballpoint, trace over the pencil lines. Add more details.

● Now color the drawing with colored markers. To finish off, you may want to erase the pencil marks that still show.

● Another way to find out how different tools work is to make several drawings of the same item, choosing a different tool for each one—a pencil, a pen, a felt pen, a charcoal stick, a chalk pastel.

Shading

Drawing the outline of an object and adding details is just the first step in making something look real. How do you make a circle look like a ball instead of a frisbee? How do you make a ball look as heavy as a boulder or as light as a balloon? The artist must make the object look as though it takes up three-dimensional space, or has volume, and has real weight, or **mass**. This is done by adding shading.

Shading shows how light affects objects. If the light comes from just one place, such as a spotlight in a dark room, it creates a highlight where it shines on the object. Where the light does not reach the object, a shadow is found. The less light there is, the deeper the shadow.

Because dark things look heavier than light-colored things, shading can be used to give the effect of weight. Compare the two circles, one black and one white.

Shading is also used to create the effect of three dimensions. Compare the two circles below. The first circle is flat; the second circle looks like a ball with a light shining on it.

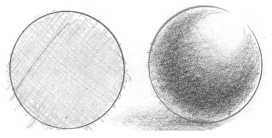

The shading of the curved surface on a ball or a can passes from light to dark very gradually. To achieve this effect, you can smudge charcoal or chalk with your finger or a piece of tissue or paper towel. Some artists use a tool called a **stump**, made from a roll of paper. You might want to buy one at an art store, or make one yourself.

Exploring Shadows

One way to make an object look solid and three-dimensional is to show the shadow it casts. Take a simple object such as a mug, a baseball or an orange. Place it in front of you on a table. Make sure there is a single source of light (a lamp or a window) just above your eye level, so that the top of the object is highlighted and the object casts a shadow.

Using charcoal, chalk or a soft

pencil, draw the outline of the object. Now observe the shadows that are on both the object and the table. If the table is light colored, you'll probably notice that some of that lightness is reflected back onto the shaded part of the object. Draw the shadows.

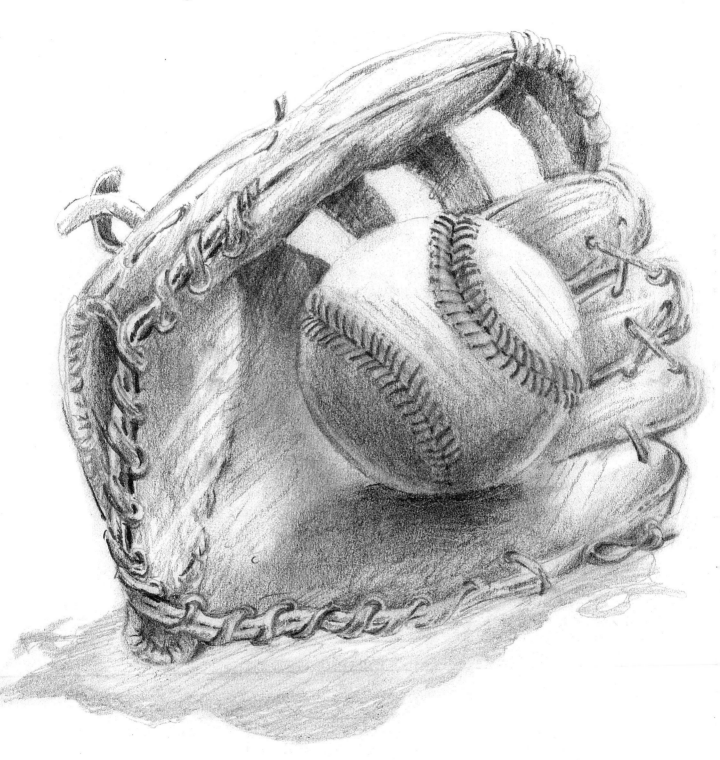

Texture

When you walk around your house, you can touch different objects and feel their texture—the woolly roughness of the carpet, the shiny smooth surface of the fridge, the silky skin of a peach. But you cannot feel these things in a picture. In a drawing, the only true texture is the feel of the paper on which the picture is drawn.

To make an object look more real, the artist has to suggest texture using techniques such as stippling and hatching. **Stippling** is done with the point of a pencil or pen or by dabbing the end of a bristle brush on the paper to make many little dots close together. **Hatching** consists of drawing many lines parallel to each other, and then many more parallel lines across the first set. Experiment with different ways of doing this in your sketchbook. Try using curved lines instead of straight ones, or make the lines very closely spaced, or vary the angles at which the two sets of lines cross.

Creating Textures

Artists create the effect of texture in many different ways. If you flip through a few art books or magazines, you'll probably find paintings and drawings that show textures in detail. Look at the kinds of brush strokes or pencil marks the artist used to create the effect of fuzzy woollen clothing, the lumpy bark of a tree, a rough brick or stone wall. Study black-and-white cartoons in the newspaper, clothing sketches in the fashion section, and drawings of different products in the advertising section.

Now see if you can reproduce some of the textural effects using pencil, felt pen or ink. Notice how the effect changes when you use different tools. Draw a broadloom rug, a piece of bread, a sponge, a woven basket, a pane of shiny glass (check a hardware catalogue or the comics page to see how artists suggest the smooth surface of glass).

Collecting Textures

Sometimes the surface underneath the drawing paper can be used to create a textured effect. Place a piece of rough sandpaper under your paper, then draw on the paper with pencil using heavy pressure. Can you see the dots left by the sandpaper?

Find other surfaces with interesting textures, like the sole of a shoe, a corrugated pizza box, a piece of window screen or a coin. Put a sheet of paper on top of each surface and rub the paper with a pencil, charcoal, chalk or crayon. Label the examples and keep them in a file folder for future reference. How could you use or copy some of these effects in your drawings? Maybe the window screen texture looks like rough brickwork. Perhaps the corrugated cardboard makes lines that look like rippling water. Experiment.

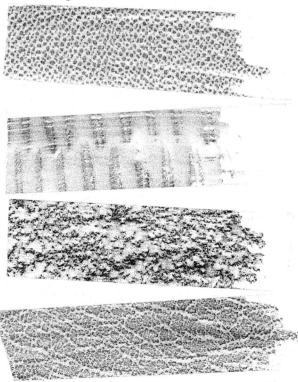

3
Using Color

Paints

In this chapter we'll explore the materials of the painter, and some of the ways artists use color.

If you go into an art supply store, you'll see shelves and rows of different kinds of painting materials (and some of them are extremely expensive!). Don't panic. All a painter needs to start is a wedge-shaped bristle brush, some poster paints in block, powder or liquid form (block paints are cheaper), old saucers or trays for mixing the paints, and newsprint paper or cartridge paper (thick drawing paper) to paint on.

There are many different kinds of paints. **Watercolor paint** is pigment mixed with a kind of glue that "binds" the pigment to the paper when it is mixed with water and spread with a brush. **Poster paints** are watercolors with "body color"

added, so that when the paint is applied, it is opaque—you can't see the paper beneath it, the way you can with watercolors.

Both watercolors and poster paints dry quickly. But in the case of **oil paints**, the pigment is mixed with linseed or poppyseed oil, which dries slowly. This allows the artist to make changes in the work before it dries, simply by wiping off the paint. Oil paintings are usually done on canvas, wood or masonite panels, rather than on paper.

Acrylic paint is a water-based paint that is transparent when mixed with water, but opaque when used straight from the tube. This means you can use it on paper like watercolors or on canvas like oil paints.

Although poster paints are good for practicing, eventually you will probably want to invest in acrylic or oil paints. They cost more, but they contain more pigment and they come in a greater variety of colors.

Brushes

Paint can be spread in many ways. It can be poured, thrown, squirted or sprayed; it can be applied with a sponge, stick, roller, fingers, feet or a raw potato.

The usual way to apply paint to paper, however, is with a brush. And just as there are different kinds of paints, there are different kinds of brushes:

● Brushes with soft, flexible hair are good with watercolors and provide a fluid, flowing effect.

● Brushes with stiff bristles are usually used with poster paint. They make firm, thick lines. You can use a dry brush technique (see pages 22 and 23) for stippling.

● Acrylic paints require nylon brushes, which must be washed in water immediately after use. (Acrylic paint is impossible to clean out of a brush or your clothes once it dries.) Because of their flexible bristles, nylon brushes can also be used with watercolors or oil paints.

Brushes come in various sizes and shapes. Wedge-shaped brushes allow you to paint thin lines as well as covering broad areas. If you are starting with poster paints, it is useful to have two brushes—a small round-tipped soft-hair brush for fine details and a larger wedge-shaped stiff-bristled one for covering broad areas.

Like paints, brushes come in a range of prices. The better ones are more expensive and require more care, but it is easier to paint the strokes you want with them.

The famous American painter Jackson Pollock painted huge canvases by pouring, spattering or even throwing the paint at the canvas. Pollock was interested in the action and energy that went into the making of art. His richly colored, thickly textured canvases came to be described as "Action Painting."

Experimenting with Paint

You'll need a large jar of water for cleaning your brushes, and at least three trays (use foil pie plates or plastic margarine containers). You'll also need a plate or tray to mix the paints on. Have a rag or paper towels handy to soak up extra water, and spread newspaper around to keep paint off the floor. (Although poster paints are usually washable, there are exceptions.) It's a good idea to keep your work area tidy and organized (although it cannot be said that all artists are neat!).

In one tray mix a tiny bit of paint with lots of water. This is called a **wash**. In the second tray mix paint and water together to the consistency of a milkshake. In the third tray mix just enough water with the paint to make it spreadable—like paste. This consistency is called **dry brush**.

Use the brushes you have to paint different kinds of strokes:
● Cover large areas with a broad brush and the thin paint mixture.
● Draw lines with the milkshake paint—thin lines, thick ones, swirling lines.
● Explore textures with the very thick paint. Blob it on, or try a stipple effect. Make patterns by using your thumb to press the paintbrush onto the paper. Date your most interesting experiments.

Sometimes you get too much paint on your paper and it makes puddles. What then?

● Dip your brush in water to clean the paint off it, then squeeze the water out of the bristles. Place the brush in the puddle to soak up the unwanted paint. Wash and squeeze the brush again and repeat until the puddle is gone.

● Very carefully, dab the puddle of paint with a tissue, sponge or paper towel. (You may even create some very interesting textures this way. Experiment!)

Papers

For painting, your paper needs to have the appropriate weight, absorbency and texture. High-quality paper is expensive, but it is worth buying when you are ready to spend more time on your painting. The paper should be heavy (thick) to keep it from wrinkling or "pooling" when the paint is added. And the paper should have **tooth**. Toothed paper is rough and soft, so it absorbs paint easily and evenly. Harder papers without tooth (like notebook paper) are sometimes used where fine lines are needed rather than color washes.

Experimenting with Papers

Find some shiny smooth paper, some regular sketching paper and some heavy watercolor paper that is very rough and textured. Mix some more paint, as you did when you were experimenting with thin and thick paint. Using different brushes, try to create the following lines, shapes and textures on each kind of paper:

● Lines that are thick and thin, straight and curved.

● Lines that start thin and straight and become thick and curved.

● Spread the bristles of your brush and use the thick paint. Make little dots (stippling) by holding your brush vertically and tapping the paper (dry brush technique).

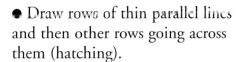

● Draw rows of thin parallel lines and then other rows going across them (hatching).

● Fill in the shapes made with the lines with solid color to create a patchwork quilt effect.

● Dip your heaviest paper in water. Try out the different effects on the wet paper. This technique is called **wet into wet**.

Color

When you are working with paint you will want to mix it to obtain lots of different colors. There are three colors that cannot be obtained by mixing, however—red, yellow and blue. These are called the **primary colors**.

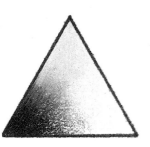

Secondary colors—orange, green and violet—are mixtures of primary colors. Mixing a primary and a secondary color produces an **intermediary color**. And colors made from earth pigments such as sienna (red plus brown) and umber (yellow plus brown) are called **tertiary colors** because they are mixtures of all three primaries. (If you mix red, yellow and blue, you get brown). **Tint** is the amount of white mixed into a color. **Tone** is the amount of black mixed into a color. Pink, for example, is a tint of red; midnight blue is a tone created by mixing blue and black.

The color triangles show these combinations.

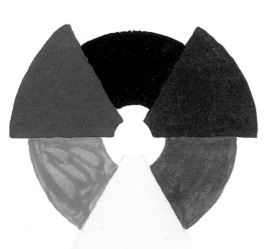

It is good to know what color combinations are possible with the paints, color pencils or pastels you have. A swatch system will give you samples of the different combinations.

Making a Swatch Collection

Cut out small pieces of white cardboard (you can also put your color samples in rows on a larger sheet). Cover the cards with color as follows:
● Card one—red
● Card two—red with a touch of blue added
● Card three—equal amounts of red and blue
● Card four—blue with a touch of red added

Always add the darker color to the lighter color. (A darker color such as blue "covers" a lighter color such as red or yellow. This means it takes more red added to blue to get violet than it does blue added to red. For this reason it is better to add a little blue to the red rather than the other way around.)

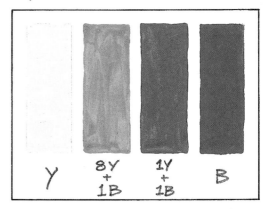

Make a second set of swatches by mixing red and yellow, and a third set by adding blue to yellow. Label each blob of color, indicating what the combinations and proportions are. Keep your swatch collection handy. When you are painting and want to produce a certain color, you

COLOR FIELD ART

Some artists paint pictures that simply show areas of plain color. These paintings have no subject and are called color field paintings. One of these artists, Josef Albers, painted colored squares against a different-colored background. Another artist, Mark Rothko, painted rectangles with fuzzy edges, so that they seemed to float within the color background. With color field paintings, the viewer is meant to enjoy the art for the interesting choices of colors, not for the subject. You can find works by Albers and Rothko in many art galleries, in art books and on postcards.

Try making your own color field paintings. Paint a square of one color within another square of a different color. The trick is to find a combination that will surprise or delight the viewer. The boundary between the two colors could be sharp and clear (hard edge), or you can make a fuzzy border where one color meets the other.

can refer to your cards to know how much of each color to mix. (You can also make cards showing tints and tones, e.g., red, red plus white, red plus black.)

Transparent Color Effects

Here's another color experiment. First, create a composition of overlapping shapes by drawing two overlapping outlines of your hands. (You could also trace overlapping leaves, or the profiles of cars, ships or airplanes.) Using paint of milkshake thickness, fill in one of the shapes with a primary color. Cover the area evenly. Fill in the second shape with a second primary color. Now fill in the overlapping area with the secondary color obtained by mixing the two primaries. This is called a "trans-

parency" effect, because it looks as though the colors are transparent, like colored glass.

3 . Using Color

Contrast

Life is full of contrasts (opposites): day and night, young and old, rich and poor, good and bad. Artists use contrasting colors or tones to make their pictures more interesting. Black used with white or red can create high contrast, or a sense of conflict. Low-contrast combinations such as gray and light blue can convey peacefulness and sadness.

Expressing Moods with Color

Colors are sometimes referred to as "warm" or "cool." Red and orange are often thought of as warm colors. Blue and green are considered cool colors. Think of phrases like "hot pink" (red plus white) or "ice blue" (blue plus white).

Warm and cool are also used to refer to emotions, so colors are often associated with feelings:

    red for anger
    green for envy
    yellow for joy
    purple for vanity
    blue for sorrow
    orange for excitement

What feelings do different colors mean to you? What colors do you like to wear? What color would you like to paint your room? Why do you think you chose these colors? Why doesn't everybody like the same colors?

You can show different feelings in a picture by using color and contrast. Try doing two pictures that convey contrasting moods.

● Choose two moods that are very different from each other, such as anger and sorrow, or excitement and loneliness. Think of themes that suggest these emotions—perhaps a storm scene for anger, a river with willow trees for sorrow, a roller coaster for excitement. You decide.

● Draw each scene on a sheet of paper.

● Color each picture with colors that you think express the mood—a storm scene could have yellow lightning, a black sky, a red barn, for example.

● When your pictures are finished, show them to friends. Is it obvious what the different moods are?

Collage

Artists use paper as a surface for a drawing or painting. But paper can also be used as a medium or a means of expression on its own. This technique is called **collage**, a French word meaning "gluing." Pablo Picasso, perhaps the most famous artist of the twentieth century, would cut out pieces of newspaper, old railway tickets, menus, programs and scraps of material and glue them onto a background surface. He did this, he said, to increase the sense of reality in his art by using actual materials from the "real" world rather than just drawing pictures of them.

Henri Matisse was another famous artist who made collages. He painted papers in various solid colors, cut them into interesting shapes, and glued them to a surface "What led me to do cutouts," he said, "was the desire to link color and drawing in a single act."

The advantage of the collage technique is that you can fiddle with the position of the shapes and move them around to find an arrangement you like before gluing them down for good.

And you don't have to limit yourself to papers of various colors or textures, either. Anything that can be glued down can be used in collage— Popsicle sticks, bottle tops, sandpaper, tin foil, or even sand or sawdust or bits of old clothing. (Just make sure your background paper is very sturdy, especially if you're gluing

heavy items.) You can even paint the objects (before or after they are glued down) to disguise their original identity. Collages are loose and free, and the results may surprise you. You'll end up with a highly textured or "tactile" work of art that can be interesting for how it feels as well as how it looks.

Making a Matisse Collage

● Paint a number of sheets of watercolor paper with flat color of medium (milkshake) thickness—not too thin, not gooey. Use one color for each sheet. Experiment with different color mixes as you did when you were making your swatch collection. You can also use colored paper or

English artist David Hockney has used the collage technique of Picasso and Matisse by cutting, overlapping and gluing photographs instead of paintings.

magazine pages instead of coloring the paper yourself.

● On separate pieces of paper, draw a variety of simple shapes based on a theme—perhaps fish and seaweed for an underwater theme, or different kinds of trees, or profiles of cars or buildings. (Make sure the shapes are very simple, otherwise they may be difficult to cut out.)

● Cut out these drawings and trace their outlines onto the colored paper, then cut out the shapes. Save the background paper as well as the shapes you have cut from it.

● Arrange the cutout shapes on a piece of construction paper or cardboard. Overlap where you wish, or use the negative or background shapes if you like.

● When you have an arrangement you like, glue down the cutouts.

Henri Matisse was a great artist who succeeded in spite of poor health. He started doing art when his mother gave him an artist's kit while he was recovering from appendicitis. In later years he was often confined to a wheelchair or bed, but he continued to make cutouts and sometimes, using a brush attached to a long stick, to paint. Shortly before his death in 1954 he said, "All my organs are sound. Only my batteries are flat. Yet my potential for creativity is still there intact." Art can be a lifelong activity.

One jewelry designer saves glossy pictures from seed catalogues and cuts and glues them to make envelopes to package her jewelry in. Another artist saves old greeting cards, magazines and advertising flyers. She glues words and pictures onto folded pieces of colored paper to make her own personalized greeting cards.

4

Drawing People

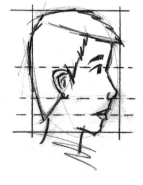

People are hard to draw because they keep moving and have a lot of parts. You can't draw a person as easily as you can draw a toaster or a piece of fruit. Your first people drawings may look more like aliens than anything else, but don't get discouraged. Drawing people is a challenge for everybody and, if you look through some art books, you'll see that some artists are better at it than others. But you'll be surprised at how much you can improve, with practice.

Drawing Faces

The most important part of a person is the face. Although every human face is different, they are all constructed in much the same way. This means that when you draw a face, you can follow certain guidelines regarding the positions of the features. If you study photographs and people around you (try to study people who don't mind being stared at!), you'll see that every face has two parts, the top (cranial) and the bottom (facial). The eyes are always placed about halfway up the head, where the two parts meet. The mouth is about halfway between the nose and the bottom of the chin.

Drawing a Self-Portrait
One face that you know very well is your own. Try drawing portraits of yourself by looking in a mirror or studying a favorite photograph.

Observe carefully the position of your eyes, nose, mouth and ears.

You might start your sketch by drawing the outside contour of your face. Then add your features, noting carefully their position and shape.

You will probably end up making several drawings. Each drawing should be fairly large (about lifesize), nearly filling your sketch pad sheet. Some details—like the pupils of the eyes—are so small that they would be impossible to draw in small scale.

Try to draw your face in three poses—front view (frontal), angular view (three-quarter) and side view (profile).

Now try to draw your face using different tools—a pencil, a felt pen, a crayon. How could you add shading with the pen by stippling or hatching? Why would a drawing in crayon or oil pastel have few details?

David Hockney is an artist who has done many drawings and paintings of himself and his family. Sometimes he does self-portraits from the waist up, even showing the pencil in his hand. Most of his works are very simple. They have a few essential lines and some shading and just a few details, such as glasses or a striped shirt.

Making Faces

● From posters, sports cards, newspapers or magazines, cut out faces that have been photographed from different angles. Draw these faces, trying to make the drawings look like the photographs. Don't exaggerate or change the features (see the section on cartooning for that). Instead, observe their actual proportions and relationship to each other. You might notice that your favorite video star

actually has quite a long nose, or that the eyes of a star athlete are closer together than most people's. Notice as many details as you can. Are the lips full or thin? Is the person's face lined or smooth?

● Try drawing a "real" face other than your own. Perhaps a family member or a friend will pose for you. (Drawing a grownup who is watching TV may be considerably easier than drawing your little sister or brother, so choose a cooperative subject!) You'll find that when you draw

a real person, you have to pay closer attention to details than when you draw a picture from a photograph, because real faces are three-dimensional. You can also choose your point of view (from the front, from an angle, from the side) rather than copying the view in the photograph.

● We look at people's expressions to tell whether they are happy or sad, angry or puzzled. When artists draw faces, they try to show these emotions, too. Observe the faces of the people around you. How do their faces change when they look happy, sad or angry? What happens to their mouths, their eyes, their foreheads? Draw a face with different expressions.

● Study the features of people on television. (You may be able to concentrate on their expressions better if you turn off the sound.) Try to draw the same face with different expressions. If you have a VCR, you can record a face and then press the Pause button to give yourself more time.

Robert Bateman, a very successful nature artist, has said that he sometimes tries to hold his face in the expression of the animal he's painting, to help him get a good likeness. He also looks at his partly completed work in a mirror on occasion to give him a fresh perspective.

In spite of all her skill, Beatrix Potter was never confident drawing people. "My brother is sarcastic about the figures," she wrote, as she was struggling to improve the drawing of Mr. and Mrs. McGregor in Peter Rabbit. *"I never learnt to draw humans."*

Drawing Figures

As with faces, no two people are built exactly the same, but there are still certain guidelines that you can follow when you are drawing human bodies. First, you will notice that the torso of the body is divided at the waist into two main parts—the rib block and the hip block. The distance from the collar bone to the top of the head is another unit of about the same length or slightly less. From the highest point on the inside of the leg to the foot makes up one half of the total height, and the leg is divided into two more or less equal parts at the knee. The distance across the shoulders is about the same as the distance from the shoulder to the elbow, and from the elbow to the wrist.

There are many ways to draw the human figure. You'll eventually decide which techniques work best for you, but in the beginning it is useful to explore some of the methods other artists have used.

As you experiment with different techniques, think of your drawings as practice exercises, rather than as finished works of art. Don't bother to erase a line you don't like. Instead, use the misplaced line as a guide to where the line should be. Use an unsuccessful drawing as a reminder of what not to do next time. (You may build up a large collection of reminders!)

You can practice drawing figures of any kind. If you have a friend who likes to draw, the two of you can take turns posing and being the subject. Choose a position that is easy to hold if you are going to be posing for a long time. (You can dress up in special clothes such as a cowboy hat or long skirt or cape to add interest and character to your pose.) Or perhaps members of your family will stay still long enough for you to draw them when they are reading a book or at the computer.

You'll probably like some of your drawings better than others. Pin these up where you can study them for a while. What is it that makes these drawings more successful? The shape of the line? The placement on the

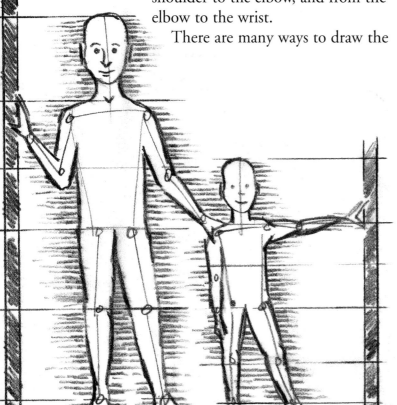

page? How can you combine the most successful elements in your next drawing? Try different ways of drawing figures. Draw from pictures in magazines or from real people.

Creatures from Boxes

It has been said that all forms in art

are derived from the circle, the square and the triangle. Using simple shapes to build up drawings of people, animals or imaginary creatures is a method that has been used by artists for a long time.

Experiment with making human figures from simple geometric shapes:
- oval for head
- rectangle for chest
- square for lower body
- thin rectangles for arms and legs
- small rectangles for hands and feet

Try making several figures of different sizes, in different poses. Study comics and cartoons and make simplified drawings of your favorite characters using geometrical shapes.

Outline Drawing

To do an outline or contour drawing, look at the subject rather than the paper. Without lifting your pencil from the paper, draw the outline of the person or animal. Sketch around the edge of the subject, noting each detail, crease or fold as you work. Try to imagine that the pencil is actually moving along the edge of the figure. Do not worry if your drawing seems to be out of proportion. In this kind of drawing it is the edge that is important.

Contour drawings help you to observe the shape of the line in your subject. To finish your sketch, add details to the outline. Remember, this kind of drawing is for practice, not for display.

Build-up Method: Drawing a Dog

Start by drawing the backbone—the line that supports the dog's body. The legs and the neck are basically shaped like cylinders, and the head is a sphere with a cylinder-shaped snout attached to it. Draw these items next. Then add details like the eyes, nose and mouth.

Once you have drawn some dogs, try other animals.

Weight Drawing

In weight drawing, you try to draw the whole form from the inside out. Weight drawings emphasize the solidity of the object rather than the outside appearance.

As you draw, feel as if you are working backward and forward as well as upward and downward, until you have actually filled up all the space between the center of the body and all of its surfaces—back, front and sides. As you draw, think about which parts of the figure look heaviest. Make them dark and solid. Other parts, such as head, arms and legs, are less heavy or bulky, so they should be drawn much more lightly. Imagine a very chubby person with pudgy arms and legs and a huge tummy, but with small wrists, hands and ankles.

Drawing Gestures and Actions

It is especially difficult to draw people when they are moving. Yet artists often want to draw people in action—a basketball player leaping for a shot, or a figure skater leaning into a spin—rather than just sitting still.

Gesture drawing stresses movement rather than appearance and shape. These sketches are like notes that you jot down quickly. They are often based on a quick glance you might have had of something you want to record before you forget it.

To make good gesture drawings, it's important to note what the subject is doing, and to ignore details like contour or texture. Draw rapidly in a continuous line, from top to bottom, around and around, without taking your pencil off the paper.

Once you understand what goes into gesture and weight drawings, you can create action scenes without copying from actual figures. This is especially true if you have noticed the positions of arms and legs and torsos as people move, and if you have noticed the relative size of different parts of the human body and where they bend—where the joints are.

You can combine action and weight drawing to make your own little army of stick figures—human and animal—all carrying out whatever activities you want to show.

Drawing Clothes

When you draw people, you will probably notice that their clothes do not always follow the lines of the bodies. A sweater or jacket, for instance, bunches up around the bend in a person's arm. Pants are wrinkled behind the knee. If a person is wearing a coat or a dress, it can hide the form of the body beneath.

How do you draw the folds in clothing (drapery)? Think of a mountain range. Along the top, the mountains will catch the sunlight. The sides of the slopes will be in partial shadow, and the valley will be dark with shadow.

When you shade drapery, leave the top white, make the two sides medium gray, and make the bottom dark gray, like the bottom of a valley. Blend the shades so there are no harsh lines.

Try making drawings of folded drapery with top, sides and base. Then try drawing real figures. Ask your model to wear a draped scarf, a cape or even a sheet or blanket. Or drape a blanket over a chair, or draw the curtains in your living room.

Try doing a number of different sketches, changing the way the drapery hangs each time. Remember to look carefully to see where the top, sides and base of the folds are.

5

Putting It Together

By now you have experimented with various ways of drawing objects and people. You've explored different media—pencil, chalk, pastels, paints, collage—and different effects using shading, texture and color.

Now we'll look at how these ideas and skills are combined—how artists compose pictures by bringing together lines, shapes, colors and textures using pencil, ink, chalk, pastel or paint.

Composition

Composition means "place together." It refers to the way shapes are arranged in a picture. The simplest composition is a single object in the center of a sheet of paper, like the drawings you did in Chapter 2. Now you can experiment with drawing two objects together.

Drawing Two Objects

To start with, the objects should be simple ones—maybe an apple and a banana, or a baseball and a cap, or two chess pieces. Place the smaller object on a low, light-colored table with the bigger object partly behind the smaller one. Use a spotlight or daylight so that you can easily see the shadow that is cast on the table.

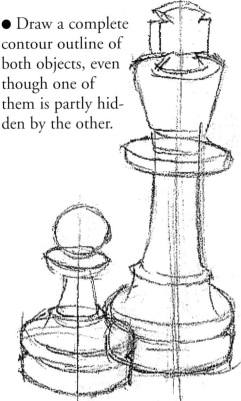

● Draw a complete contour outline of both objects, even though one of them is partly hidden by the other.

● Add details such as the stitching on the ball, the label on the bottle, the pattern on the watermelon or the rough texture on the grapefruit.

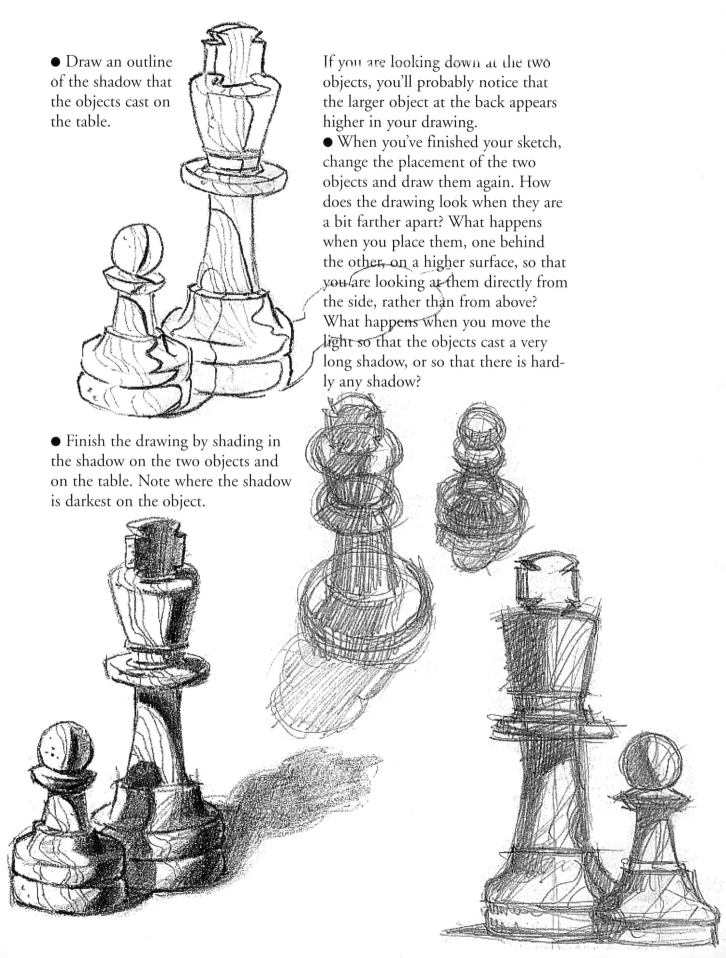

● Draw an outline of the shadow that the objects cast on the table.

If you are looking down at the two objects, you'll probably notice that the larger object at the back appears higher in your drawing.

● When you've finished your sketch, change the placement of the two objects and draw them again. How does the drawing look when they are a bit farther apart? What happens when you place them, one behind the other, on a higher surface, so that you are looking at them directly from the side, rather than from above? What happens when you move the light so that the objects cast a very long shadow, or so that there is hardly any shadow?

● Finish the drawing by shading in the shadow on the two objects and on the table. Note where the shadow is darkest on the object.

Balance

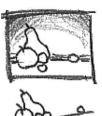

If there are two or more objects in a picture, artists usually want to make sure that the arrangement is balanced. One part of the picture should not look too heavy in comparison with the other parts.

To decide whether a picture is in balance, imagine that there is a little seesaw under it. Looking at the size, color, shape, texture and arrangement of all the things in the picture, you can decide whether the two sides of the art balance out.

Artists also like to give each picture a **focal point**, or center of interest. Many place the focal point near, but not exactly at, the middle of the picture. These compositions can be very strong and compelling, but they can also end up being boring and dead-looking (like a bull's eye placed at the center of a circle). Try experimenting with different focal points. How does the viewer's eye travel around the picture, and where does it end up?

In composing a picture, artists often think of a major horizontal line, such as the line of the horizon, and one or two major vertical lines

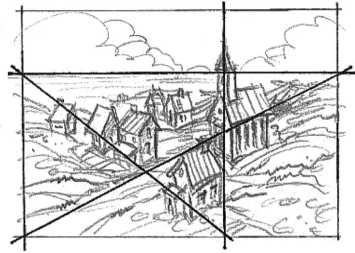

When two sides of a picture form a mirror image of each other, the kind of balance produced is called **bilateral symmetry**. A goalie's net or an automobile seen from the front are bilaterally symmetrical. So is a human being.

There are other kinds of symmetry, too. With **radial symmetry**, lines radiate from the center, like the spokes of a wheel or dart board. A tornado or whirlpool viewed from above, the spider at the center of its web, or a pane of glass that has just been shattered by a speeding bullet are all examples of radial symmetry.

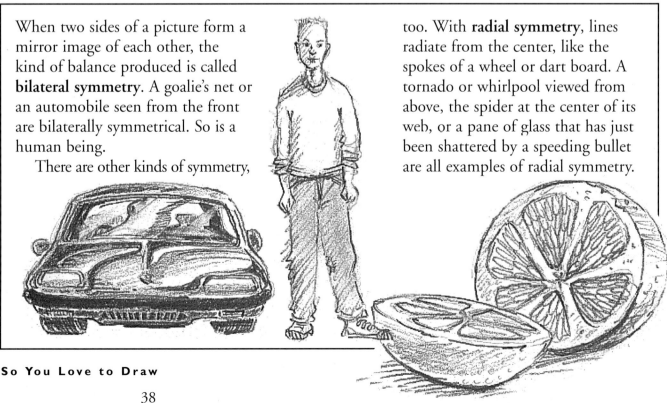

(buildings, trees, mountains) to act as a kind of frame for the focal point. Nature is not necessarily arranged like this, but an artist can choose a particular slice of it to draw, the same way a photographer chooses a scene to photograph. This slice would have a main horizontal and vertical component, a strong subject and balance. You can make a small frame to help you focus on a particular scene. You can also make quick sketches—called **thumbnail sketches** because they are very small—to experiment with different arrangements. The frame helps you concentrate on an arrangement that already exists in nature. The thumbnails let you invent your own arrangement.

Making a Compositional Frame

Cut a frame from a piece of cardboard. Make the width of the hole in the frame about two-thirds as long as the length. You could also experiment with frames of different proportions. Try a frame with a square hole in it, or a long skinny frame that could be used horizontally to view a distant vista, or vertically to frame trees, a waterfall or tall buildings. Remember that pictures do not all have to be the same shape.

To use your frame, hold it at arm's length.

Look through it to the scene beyond. Move it slowly as you watch the scene in the frame change. Stop when you find an arrangement that you think might make an interesting picture.

Playing with Thumbnails

On a sheet of sketch paper, make a number of thumbnail sketches in which you arrange trees and houses on a street, flowers in a garden or knights in a battlefield (use gesture drawing for the figures). Try a different arrangement in each sketch:

- one where vertical lines are stressed and the horizon is not prominent (perhaps trees in a forest, or an ant's view of blades of grass)
- one in which the horizontal lines are stressed, and there are few verticals (perhaps the sun setting across the sea or racing cars on a raceway)

- one where there is a very strong focal point, framed by both vertical and horizontal accents (perhaps a building on a cliff or a pair of jeans on a clothesline).

Unity in Variety

Have you ever noticed that some days there is simply too much to do? Too much homework to get done in too little time, hockey practice at the same time as the basketball game, twelve pizza toppings to choose from. There are too many choices, and we can become confused and frustrated. Then some days there is no choice. The teacher gives you exactly the same work as the day before, you've had macaroni three nights in a row, the TV shows are all reruns. Everything is the same, and life is boring.

The same is true of drawings and paintings. Some pictures just do not have enough in them to make them interesting. A picture shows a cottage by a lake in the woods: the cottage is brown, and so is the forest. The painting looks like a photograph of the same subject. It is nice, but it is not exactly exciting.

Other pictures may have so much happening that they are confusing, like those puzzle pictures where you have to find the little man in the striped shirt amidst thousands of other objects. There is no focal point, no place for the eye to rest.

A composition is usually more

attractive to people if they can see clearly what it is a picture of and how the different parts of the picture relate to each other. These pictures have enough happening to be interesting but not so much as to appear cluttered, so that the main point of the composition is lost. The idea of reaching a balance between too much and too little is called **unity in variety**.

Boring vs. Chaotic

Try doing three compositions:

● Make one drawing plain and simple—perhaps a house on a hill or a ship on a flat, empty sea. There are no clouds or birds in the sky, no flowers, trees or paths near the house, no waves in the water. Use just one drawing tool for this picture.

● Make another drawing that is as full of things as you can manage—houses, trees, birds and airplanes flying through clouds at sunset, mountains in the background, a highway cutting across the page and so on.

Use as many different kinds of tools and colors as you can for this one.

● Finally, choose the most interesting ideas from your second composition. Make a third composition, more varied than the first and less chaotic than the second. Which picture do you like best? (Your choice may depend on what kind of day you've had!)

Creating Tension

Tension is what you feel when a piece of china flips out of your hand and crashes to the floor, and you hear the sounds of a parent coming downstairs. It is intense suspense. It is anxiety or excitement.

There is a lot of tension in sports. Which of the two evenly matched teams will tilt the balance and win the game? Will a swimmer or skier set a new record?

Artists like to create tension in their paintings, too, by arranging colors, shapes and lines in a certain way.

Power Pictures

You can do this activity on your own or with a friend.

● Choose two simple shapes, such as a circle and a diamond. Choose a different color for each shape.

● Cut out two small circle shapes, two medium-sized ones and two large ones from one colored sheet of paper. Cut out small, medium and large diamond shapes using the second color.

● Cut out twelve long, skinny shapes from a sheet of black paper.

● Place the shapes one at a time on a large sheet of white paper. Start with a circle, then a black line, a diamond, a black line, etc. After each placement, ask yourself which color and shape dominate the space. Which shape do you look at first? Where does your eye end up? What happens when shapes overlap?

● When all the shapes and lines have been used, glue them down.

● There are many variations to this exercise. Use different shapes and colors. Try cutting out curved or squiggly lines instead of straight ones. Experiment with different-colored backgrounds.

Style

The word style refers to the way something looks or how it is done, rather than what it is. Some styles are neat, symmetrical and logical. Some are loose and emotional.

Every artist develops his or her own style. Emily Carr, a painter who lived from 1871 to 1945, painted the British Columbia rainforest, tackling her canvases with huge brush strokes. She liked to convey movement and freedom in her paintings. Mary Pratt, an East Coast artist, has a different style. She likes to paint closeup views of things around the house—the roast in the oven, eggs in a bowl, salmon on tin foil—and she uses photographs as sources for her images.

6
Making Pictures

Depth and Perspective

If you look out your window, you will notice that faraway things appear smaller than things that are close to you, even when they are really the same size. A truck, for instance, will look smaller and smaller as it drives off into the distance.

Artists try to copy this effect when they want to make one object look farther away than others. One way to do this is by dividing a picture into layers, or planes, like the scenery on a stage set.

Imagine, for example, that you are standing on a hill overlooking a valley. On the far side of the valley there is a row of hills with trees along them. Beyond the hills, and partly hidden by them, is a lake. On the other side of the lake lie distant mountains.

There are five layers in this scene: 1) the edge of the hill where you are standing, 2) the valley floor, 3) the hills with the trees, 4) the lake and 5) the mountains beyond. The farther away the layer, the higher up it will appear on the page. The objects in the closest layers will be larger than the same objects in other layers (e.g., trees in layer one will be bigger than the trees in layer three). As well, the farther away the layers, the grayer the colors will be. The details and textures are also less clear when things are far away.

The one disadvantage of layering is that in real life, depth does not go back in steps. Instead, there is a con-

tinuous path from close to far away. Many artists use **perspective** to create a continuous sense of depth.

There are four basic rules to remember about perspective:
1) Lines in perspective are those that recede or move away from the viewer.
2) The **horizon line** is a horizontal line at the eye level of the artist or viewer.

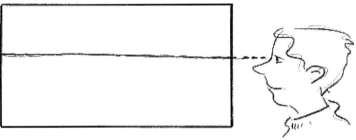

3) Lines in perspective slant down toward the horizon if they are above the artist's eye level, and upward if they are below the horizon.

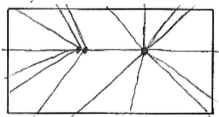

4) In perspective, parallel lines, if extended, meet at a point on the horizon line called the **vanishing point.** (Each set of parallel lines leads to its own vanishing point.)

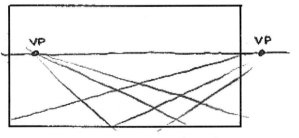

Confusing? Follow the rules of perspective by drawing a box.

Drawing a Box in Perspective

1. Draw the horizontal line.

_____

2. Draw a vertical line to form one edge of the box.

_____

3. Draw the top and bottom of one side, extended to meet at a point on the horizon line.

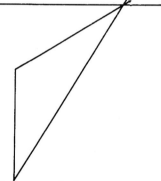

4. Draw the second side, extended to meet at a second point on the horizon line.

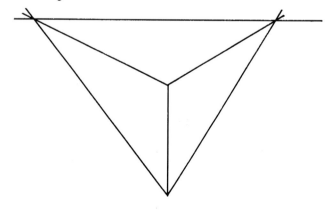

5. Draw vertical lines to show two more edges of the box.

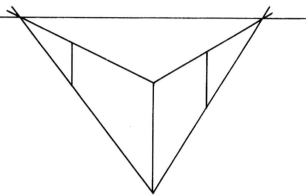

6. Draw lines from A to A1 and from B to B1. Now you can see the top of the box.

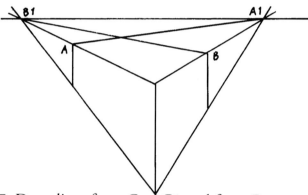

7. Draw lines from C to C1 and from D to D1. Now you have the bottom of a transparent box. Complete by joining E to E1 to create the back corner.

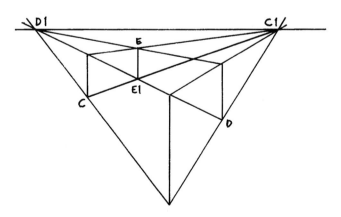

Practice making boxes of various sizes. Once you've drawn many of these, you could explore even further.

● Draw a box floating above the horizon line, so that its bottom is visible.

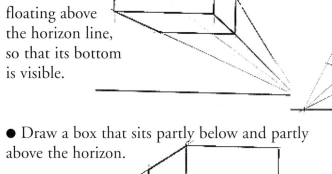

● Draw a box that sits partly below and partly above the horizon.

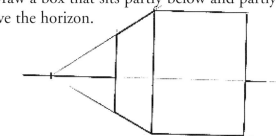

● Draw a box with a hole or window in it so that you can see part of the horizon through the hole.

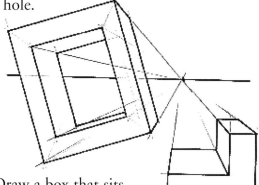

● Draw a box that sits partly in front of another box.

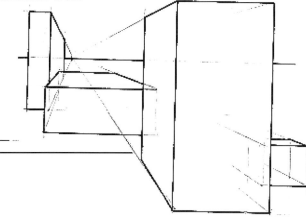

● Draw parts of boxes—perhaps the bottom and one side, or the top and the back.

For all these drawings you should always start with a horizon line, since all the perspective lines slope toward it. The construction lines can be erased once the drawing is complete. Then the sides of the boxes can be colored or textured to make them look solid.

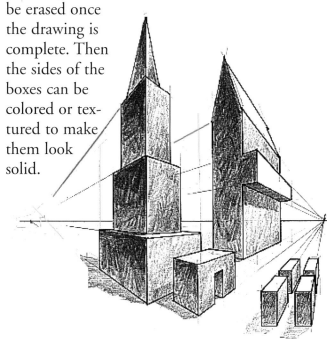

Once you can draw boxes in perspective, you can create pictures of imaginary cities, boxes of birthday gifts, cages at the zoo, or buildings with large windows showing interior spaces. You can then add people, plants, trees and other details.

Making a Cityscape

Perspective is the ideal technique to use when you're drawing scenes of a city, because of all those box-shaped buildings. A cityscape could be a downtown of a big city, or a street scene in a town or village, or completely imaginary.

To start your cityscape, draw the horizon line—the line showing eye level—even if some or all of the horizon will eventually be covered up by the buildings in front.

Put in the lines of the streets next. If the streets lead toward the horizon, their lines will meet at the vanishing point. Note that the vanishing point may be outside the picture (see below). If it is, you will need to tape your sketch pad onto a larger sheet, extend the horizon and then draw your perspective lines to the vanishing point. Or, you can imagine where the vanishing point would be and draw your perspective lines so that they point to it.

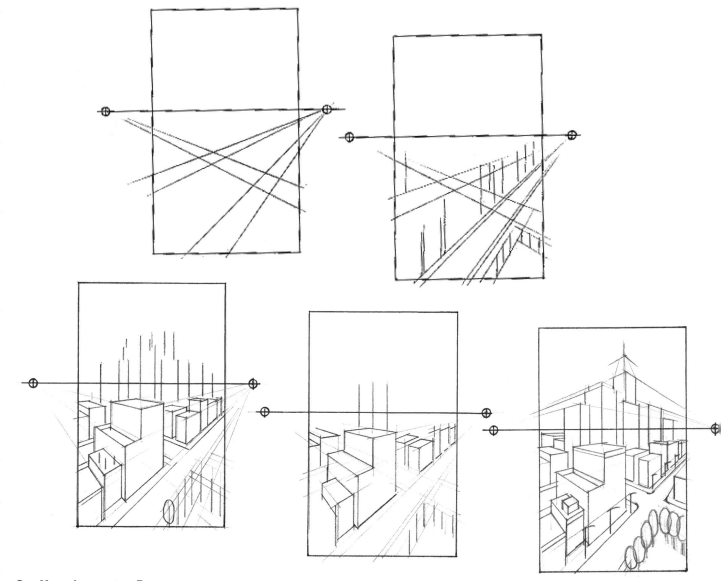

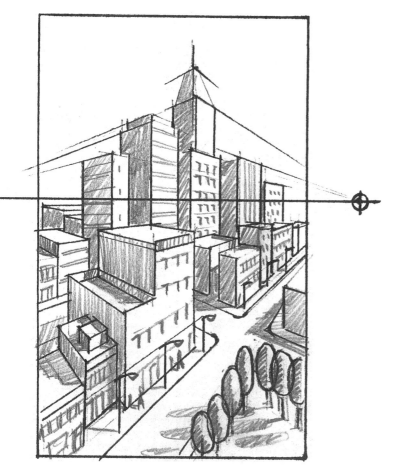

Next, draw buildings. Draw the vertical lines first, then the horizontal lines leading toward the vanishing points on the horizon line. A horizontal line above your eye level slants down toward the horizon, and those below slant up.

After you have blocked in the general shape of the buildings on the street, add details such as doors and windows, lamp posts, fire hydrants, newspaper boxes, garbage pails. If you are drawing a futuristic city, you might want to add supersonic vehicles, surveillance devices and perhaps a few one-eyed citizens as well.

If you have worked in pencil, you may want to go over top of your drawing with a pen or felt pen—or both—redrawing and strengthening lines and edges. You can add more detail, such as the patterns of the bricks, the lines of the window frames, the lettering on the signs in the store windows.

Finally, you can add color. A little color and lots of water—a color wash—could be used for the sky, the buildings and the road. Thicker color could be added to show details such as people, lamp posts or objects in the store windows. Artists sometimes use stronger colors like red to emphasize objects in the foreground, and cool colors like green and blue for distant objects.

6. Making Pictures

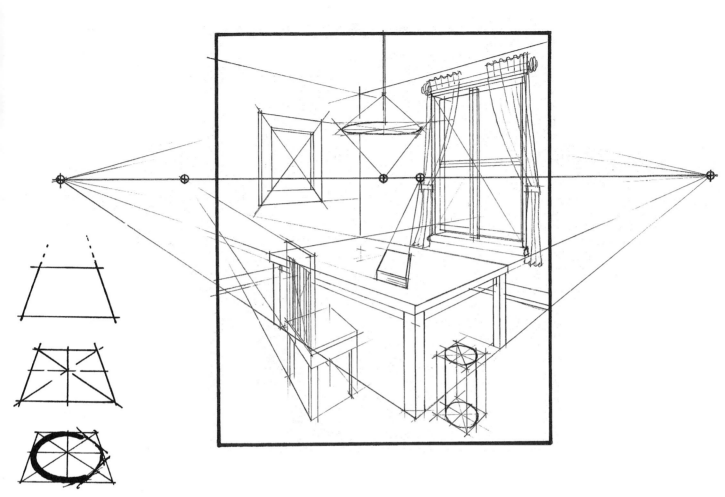

Perspective is well suited to making boxes and buildings, but the world has curved lines in it as well. One way to draw curves is to draw a square in perspective, then draw a circle inside that square.

Inside in Perspective

Perspective can also be used to make interior scenes more realistic.

Draw the corner of a room. Start by lightly drawing the horizon line at your eye level. Unless there is a window facing the horizon, this line will not appear in the final drawing.

A chair or table in the room will probably be below your eye level (unless you are sitting on the floor), so you will draw the rectangle of the upper surface, with parallel lines converging slightly to meet at a point on the horizon line. Note that each object may have its own set of vanishing points.

After you have "blocked in" the walls, windows, pictures, tables and chairs, you can add details.

When you have finished, compare your drawing with the corner of an actual room. You may notice that the angles of the real room look less steep. That's because in real life the vanishing points are much farther apart than you may have shown them in your drawing.

Landscapes

You can draw landscapes by actually going to the countryside or the sea-side, sitting down in front of a nice view and drawing what you see. But you can also draw a scene you remember—maybe the view of the lake from a summer campsite, or a scene that you saw from a car or a bus window. Or you can look at landscapes in paintings, photographs, postcards, magazines, calendars or posters.

The great thing about being an artist is that you don't have to copy exactly what you see. Instead, artists use "artistic license" to make their compositions more interesting. You can even combine several scenes and memories to create a landscape no one has ever seen before. You can imagine the most beautiful piece of property in the world, with the perfect beach, hills for skiing in winter, a pond for skating, forests for walking. The possibilities are endless.

Judging Landscape Pictures for Balance

Look at landscapes that have been photographed or painted by someone else. Analyze these pictures by putting a sheet of tracing paper over them. With a ruler and pencil, trace the main vertical (buildings, trees, mountains, etc.) and horizontal (horizon line) elements.

● What are the major vertical and horizontal elements? Where do they divide the composition? Is the horizon line near the bottom of the picture, near the top, exactly halfway? What effect does this create?

● Is the focal point near the center of the composition or off in a corner? How is the viewer's eye led to it?

● Imagine that the picture is sitting on an imaginary seesaw (see page 38). Are the various elements—subject, textures and colors, lines and shapes—balanced?

When you are planning your own landscape pictures, you might try sketching several thumbnail versions, moving trees or lamp posts, placing the horizon at different levels, moving the tree line or the low hills up or down.

After you have done a number of thumbnails, choose the one you like best for the final composition.

the painting is done, the medium used, and what the artist wishes to emphasize.

Choose a scene close to where you live, perhaps a ravine or park near your home, or even your backyard. Make this *your* scene. Draw it often. Use different media. Move things around if you like. Show how the scene changes at different times of the day or year. Draw it from different angles, from up close and far away. Make a collection called "the view near my studio" or "the field behind the house."

The French painter Claude Monet was famous for painting the same scene many times. His pictures of London Bridge from dawn to dusk are so accurate that they have been photographed and made into a short movie that shows the changes of light, shadow and color on the bridge throughout the day.

Exploring Landscapes

Some artists spend their whole lives working on landscape sketches and paintings, because there are so many different kinds of landscapes. The same scene can look very different depending on the time of day, the weather, the viewpoint from which

Mixing Media

The artist's tool, medium and surface all affect the appearance of the final artwork. A face drawn with a jumbo crayon on construction paper will look very different from the same face drawn with pen and ink on drawing paper.

Sometimes you may want to mix media. Comic-book illustrators, for example, often use pencil to make their original sketches and then use ink over top to strengthen the lines and shapes. Then they add paint inside the lines for color. Sometimes a different illustrator is responsible for each step.

Illustrators of children's books often mix media, too. Take a look at several picture books to see if you can identify which techniques the artists have used.

Different Media, Different Effects
● Choose a subject that includes objects requiring well-defined lines—perhaps fruit on a table or cars in a parking lot.
● On a sheet of sketching paper, draw the subject lightly in pencil, outlining the basic shapes. Don't bother filling in all the details.

● Outline and fill in some of the foreground objects with oil pastel. Press hard (but not so hard that you break the pastel).

● Using the same pastels, add some color and detail within these shapes.

● Mix a wash of watercolor (much water and little paint). With a large brush, fill in background areas such as the tabletop or wall behind the fruit, or the sky or parking lot surface.

● Mix wet paint to the consistency of a milkshake and paint over top of the objects you detailed in pastel. The paint should wiggle off the pastel, fill the gaps between and leave a mottled effect. Experiment with different effects by changing the thickness of the pastel lines, and the thickness of the paint.

Imaginary Worlds

Artists often draw what they imagine, rather than what they see. But no matter how different imagined worlds are from the "real" world, they are usually still based on the world we all live in and observe. A spacescape, for instance, may have homes that look like giant beehives; aliens might still have limbs and heads and eyes.

No matter where your imaginary landscape is set, it will look more real if you use the principles of perspective. If you do not, your world may look fantastic, more dream-like.

How do you create an imaginary world? To start, choose the following things:
- a time of day—dawn, noon, sunset, night
- a season of the year—fall, winter, spring, summer
- weather conditions—tornado, drizzle, fog, sunshine, snow, soft mist
- a place or setting—inner city, farm, forest, desert
- a location—in the air, on the ground, underground, under the sea
- population—many, few, humans, animals, birds, imagined
- artifacts—buildings, vehicles, equipment
- a subject—this can be a single dramatic event such as jumping off a bridge at night, or a scene, such as a garden of fantastic flowers or a view of paradise

Before composing the picture of your imaginary world, you might want to do a number of quick drawings showing portions of it: the kinds of plants, the look of the sky, the kinds of objects you would find there. Try to combine these things in a number of rough sketches. How would your vehicle look if it was partly hidden

Creating an Imaginary Creature

There are a number of ways to create imaginary creatures and imaginary settings:

● Scribble randomly, using a felt pen on an ordinary piece of paper. Now look for combinations of lines that might suggest limbs or eyes or ears or wings. Copy the outlines of these parts onto a body or torso that you make up. Redraw the parts until you have a creature that you like.

● Close your eyes and draw a picture —either what you see in your imagination, or simply let your hand wander over the picture. Open your eyes. See if you can find the beginnings of a creature in what you have drawn. Emphasize or exaggerate the parts that will make the creature more life-like and interesting.

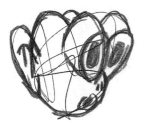

● Make some sketches of things you might not usually think of drawing—the pattern of clouds, blobs of paint spilled on the floor. Add arms, legs, fins, tails, eyes or antennae to any of these to make a strange creature.

● Imagine how your creature might live. What does it eat? How does it move? Where does it sleep? What kinds of teeth, limbs and body would it have to allow it to do these things? A wide mouth suitable for eating potato chips whole? Big flat feet so it can sleep standing up?

Think Small!

There is a fantastic world waiting to be discovered, but it is almost too small to see. Find a magnifying glass and go exploring. Then try drawing some of these things in your sketchbook. They could be the basis for a world of alien creatures.

● swirling lines, deep crevices and tall spiky hairs on the back of your hand
● fantastic patterns on pansy petals
● big boulders made out of Rice Krispies
● filmy lace on the wing of a moth

People like to draw because it's a great way to use your imagination and express yourself. But art has many practical purposes, too.

Illustration

An illustration is a story-telling picture. Often the story is also described in words that accompany the picture. The word "illustrate" means to explain, to make clear.

The text and its accompanying illustration should work together. Sometimes they describe an event or thing. A magazine, for example, might contain an illustrated article about a space telescope or garden plants. A story in the school yearbook might describe the day the school football team beat the current champions.

GOT ANY FRESH WORMS?

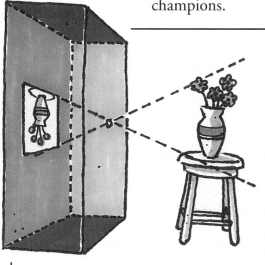

For centuries artists have used mechanical aids to help them draw more realistically. In the fifteenth century the *camera obscura* was a box that projected an image onto a screen so the artist could trace it in a larger size.

Many commercial illustrators use an air brush, which uses compressed air to blow a fine mist of paint onto a surface. Because the color sprays can be blended, it can create realistic tones and shading.

Finally, computers have extended the possibilities for artists even more. Some artists work on computer monitors, either to create still figures or animated ones. Other computer artists input designs or pictures and mix them with their own artwork to create a collage.

Illustrating a Nature Guide

Imagine that you have been asked to prepare a page for a guide to wildflowers in your area.

● Choose a flower or a plant that grows near your home.

● In an encyclopedia or flower guide, find out some information about this plant—its name, the names of its parts, its life history from seed to maturity.

● Type or print out a short description of the plant.

Rose: (ROSA)
There are many kinds of

● On a piece of paper, make a detailed sketch of the whole plant. On separate pieces of paper, make smaller sketches of individual parts of the plant, such as a leaf or a petal, showing the shape, the veining and the color. Add labels with arrows pointing to the plant's features.

● Arrange the description of the plant and your illustrations on a page of your sketchbook. Try to make the arrangement look balanced (see page 38), making sure your page is clear and not cluttered. Add rules or boxes if you like.

● When you have an arrangement you like, paste down the text and drawings. Add a title. Finish your sketch with colored pencils, paints or pastels if you like.

● Instead of a plant, you might want to describe and draw a piece of machinery, such as a bicycle or a camera, or perhaps something more fantastic, like a cottage built on the bottom of a lake.

David Hockney has two large photocopy machines in his studio in Los Angeles. He uses them to copy everything in sight—leaves, maps, grass, towels, shirts. He uses these images as raw material for his art.

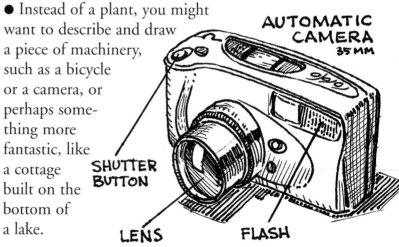

AUTOMATIC CAMERA 35 MM

SHUTTER BUTTON

LENS

FLASH

7. Exploring Further

59

In her book,
Extra! Extra!
Linda Granfield
interviews Lynn
Johnston, creator
of the comic strip
For Better or For
Worse. *Johnston*
gives these tips to
young people who
like to draw
comic strips:
- *Practice a lot.*
- *Copying isn't bad unless you say someone else's work is yours.*
- *Develop your own style. A cartoonist's style is as personal as his or her signature.*
- *Learn from others by studying your favorite artists.*
- *Never say, "I'm good." Say, "I could be better."*

Drawing Comics

Cartoonists are the people who draw the characters you see in comic books, on television and in the newspaper. Cartooning is a method of drawing in which figures are simplified and distorted to bring out or exaggerate particular characteristics. Comics are stories told in a series of pictures; the characters' dialogue is often printed inside "balloons."

Looking at Comics

Look at your favorite comics. Notice how the cartoonist has drawn the outline shapes, how objects are colored (usually with flat color and little shading) or textured (with dots or lines), and how the objects, figures and word balloons are arranged in the frames. Observe how the artist draws the same figure in various poses, such as sitting down, running, leaning over, or flying through the air.

Choose one frame from a comic strip and copy it, just for practice. (Change the words in the balloon if you like, but try to keep the lettering as neat and clear as possible.)

Creating Comic Characters

Comic-strip characters can usually be identified by a few personality traits. Maybe they are strong and stupid, or mean and sly, or gentle and funny. These characteristics are often emphasized by their physical appearance.

- To invent your own comic character, first write down the kind of creature you are thinking of. Is it an alien bent on destruction? A clown with a mean streak? A clam who is shy? Fill a sheet with rough drawings of this creature. Draw it in different poses—running, sitting down, sleeping. How does its expression change when it is feeling mean? Lovable? Silly? Lonely?
- Choose the sketch you like best and redraw it, this time in full color. Draw the character's house or surroundings.
- Now repeat the process with a second character that contrasts with the first, e.g., an earthling hero to outwit the alien; a magician to hypnotize the clown and expose his sly deeds; a starfish to tease the clam.

Creating a Storyboard

A storyboard is a series of boxes or frames, each of which shows one scene of the story that is being told. There are usually three or four frames going across the page, or eight to ten frames arranged in two or three rows.

And where do ideas for stories come from? What has happened around your house lately? Or in the schoolyard? Your father using a ladder to get the family cat off the neighbor's roof? Balloons blowing away from some little kid and getting caught in some trees? The teacher blaming one student for doing something wrong, and you know who really did it? Many comic-book artists get their ideas from the things that happen to them every day.

Once you have an idea for a story, you need an ending, a surprise for the last frame, like the punch line of a joke. Something unexpected. Perhaps the ladder begins to slip and the cat, in a panic, jumps onto the father's head.

Think of a simple plot or story line for your character and show it going through the motions, one action for each frame.

Frame 1: Creature stands on a mountaintop or on the ledge of a building.
Frame 2: It looks down, frightened.
Frame 3: It looks up, thinking.
Frame 4: It sprouts wings.
Frame 5: It is gone.

Observing and Collecting

Artists are constant observers. They are always searching for good ideas to use in their own work. Because of this, most artists like to study the work of other artists.

Art books can show you many examples of work by famous artists—figure drawing and painting, landscapes, seascapes, cityscapes, paintings from the imagination, graphic design, art by illustrators, and many other kinds of art as well.

Browse through art books in your local library. Which works and artists do you especially like, and why? Do you like the way a certain artist draws people or the way someone chooses colors? Find out more about your favorite artists. You might be able to collect their pictures on postcards, calendars or in magazines.

Most artists are great collectors. They keep files full of ideas, photographs of things they might want to draw some day, reproductions of works they admire. You might want to start your own collection. You can also collect interesting objects that you would like to draw. Or you might collect different papers or other textured materials to use in a collage.

Saving and Displaying Your Work

As you work on your art, you will gradually build up a large collection of drawings and paintings. You'll probably decide that some of this work is unsuccessful and can be considered scrap. You might want to recycle it as collage material, or perhaps you can do another drawing on the other side.

Some of your work may be incomplete, or it may be only partly successful. Perhaps your dinosaur's expression is wonderfully fierce and scary, but the body looks too small and soft. A work like this should be filed. You might want to draw an expression like that again some day, and this drawing will show you how you did it before.

It's important to save the work you have done, and to keep it clean and organized. (Who knows? One day when you are famous, these early drawings could be worth a lot!) Placing tissue paper over chalk or charcoal drawings will help prevent them from smudging.

Keep your work in cardboard folders. Mark each folder with a label such as "Pencil Drawings 1996" or "Figure Drawings." Sign and date each drawing; place the drawings in the folder by order of date.

You may want to display your best work or give it away as a gift. To protect this art and set it off, you can mount it.

There are different ways to mount